Teddy boo, ban and hipo story picture book

this is pushi
cat he is
very strong

this is teddy boo is friend
with pushi cat

teddy boo and pushi cat
are boxing

this is teddy ban he is a
military officer

this is bobos he is an airforce officer, he fly aircraft to battle field

mama tiger and baby tiger and owl

teddy ban like riding a
bike

camping is fun

this is hipo he like going
to the gym to look fit

Hipo like skipping and
having fun

hipo is listening
to music and
dancing, having
fun all the
way...

captain hook the pirate

captain hook has a
cat name shu shu,
when he say shu hu
the cat say meowww.

this is the B
he like
fishing,

Meet Sam the fire fighter, anywhere there is fire out break he is there to put if off and rescue people.

this is tiga he like going
under the sea.

this is a bear
it is wild, so
never go
close

meet
cona
the stone
age man

this is tatafo the parot,
the can talk like a human
and friendly

this is zee the
dog, he is man's
best friend

dave and esther going
to school.

they are all in every aspect of life,

hope you enjoy reading this book,

have a wonderful day.

Stanley Djgbo

www.ingramcontent.com/pod-product-compliance
Lightning Source LLC
Chambersburg PA
CBHW041136260726
48664CB00027B/1260